YOU ARE THE LEGACY:

A GENERATIONAL TREE

Peggy B. Dixon

ROYSTON
Publishing

You Are The Legacy:
A Generational Tree

Peggy B. Dixon

BK Royston Publishing.
PO. BOX 4321
Jeffersonville IN 47131
502-802-5385
http://bkroystonpublishing.com
bkroystonpublishing@gmail.com

Copyright 2021 by Peggy B. Dixon

All Rights Reserved. This book is protected under the copyright laws. Contents and/or cover may not be reproduced in whole or in part in any form without the express written permission of the author, except for brief quotations or occasional page copying for personal or group study is encouraged.

Cover Design by: Elite Cover Designs

ISBN: 978-1-955063-25-8

Printed In The United States of America

DEDICATION

I am thankful ALMIGHTY GOD loved me before I was born. It is for this reason alone that I dedicate this book to HIS children all over the world so that they, too, might know HIS love and sacrifice for them.

I am thankful my husband Walter is also a recipient of ALMIGHTY GOD'S love and sacrifice. I am thankful he has been from the day we married a great example of love in my life and in our children's lives. "Thank you," is just not enough.

To my children Reesa, Cyrus (Stephanie), and Rachel Dixon and God-daughter Yashica Kearse, I am thankful for what each of you brings to my life individually and collectively.

To my amazing grandsons Darnell, Joel, and little brother Timothy, twin grandsons, Walter & Wesley, and to my grand-God daughters: MiAsia and Gia. Thank you for allowing me the opportunity to speak into your lives using this book.

I would be in great error if I didn't thank and honor my only living Aunt Anna Grevious (Richard, Sr., deceased) for your unconditional love for me. Thank you! To my living tree siblings and the memory of deceased tree siblings: Ella Veal (Donald, deceased), Vickie Powell, Vincent Carter, Alice Jackson, George Jackson (Kathy), Roderick Jackson (deceased), Jewell Jackson Brown (Adam), Donna Patton Greene (deceased), Cheryl Covington (David), Kim Stevenson (Tina), Derek Stevenson (Marcia). I honor our family ties.

To all my cousins, nieces, nephews, in-laws and friends. Family is everything. I love you.

ACKNOWLEDGMENTS

To every Apostle, Prophet, Evangelist, Pastor, and Teacher who helped me to mature as a generational tree, thank you.

To the memories of these great trees who have passed, I will be forever grateful for your wisdom, love, correction, and sacrifices that have helped to shape me:

My Grandmother:

Margret Canady Jackson,

My Parents:

George & Georgia Jackson, Sara & Robert Mundy,

Samuel Carter,

Mother in-law and Father in Law

Dorcas Rose Dixon and Wilburt Dixon

Aunts & Uncles:

Maggie Dialls, Dudley Dialls, Theda Washington, Roderick & Clara Kennedy, Claude & Frances Kennedy, Alice & Robert Lewis, Anna Gray and Richard (Julia) Gray.

I have a special place in my heart for Denise Guillain, who read the first draft some 20 years ago and has gone home to be with OUR LORD, SAVIOR, and KING.

TABLE OF CONTENTS

Dedication	iii
Acknowledgements	v
Introduction	ix
Womb of the Earth	1
The Reaction to the Light	3
Exceptional Differences	5
The Reward of Support	9
The Daily Struggles	11
Exhaustion Impedes the Vision	13
Maturity Comes with a Price, It Stands Alone	15
Salutation	19
An Awareness	27
The Purpose Behind A Move	29
Wrong Assumptions	33
Denial	35
Surface Roots	37
The Cost of a Hill	41
Make It Personable, "SING"	45
Shaking and Shifting from the Inside	49
Broken Promises	55

The Mudslinging Enemy	59
The Obvious Observation	65
Corrective Vision by a Touch	67
The Touch of the Wind	69
Protest	75
Cut Down to Size	79
The *I's* Have Finally Done It	83
The Weight of the Fight	87
Celebratory Season	93
The Markings of Truth	97
The Author	103

INTRODUCTION

When I was younger, much younger, I was called a tomboy because I could climb trees with the best of the boys in the neighborhood. I also endured just as many injuries as they did. Not once did I break my leg as a result of these jumps. However, I was whisked off to the emergency room many times for a nail or some glass stuck in my foot from jumping out of a tree and landing wrong.

Even as a young adult, I was found climbing a tree with a youth group I taught during a summer vacation Bible camp. It was my way of really connecting with the teens I had been assigned. They laughed because they thought I was too old to be climbing trees. That day I taught the lesson sitting in a tree.

However, my favorite tree memories are of the

tree that was two doors from my house. This thing was tall and it was huge. It took three to four of us to put our arms around it. The tree served as our base when we played hide and seek, tag, or home plate for baseball. We played marbles, sat, and read books, played with paper dolls, cars, trucks, and trains at the base of this tree. We tied our bikes to this tree. We sat or played with the neighbor dog Skipper, a white border collie around this tree. It was also the tree where we sat and had conversations with each other while eating lunch or ice cream cones.

This tree belonged to a living tree we called "Miss Rosie" who stood tall, as well. Something I noticed about both of these trees is the fact they had endured the pressures, challenges, and the storms of life making them trees that stood tall.

Yet these aren't the only trees that stand tall. There are an estimated nine billion living trees in the world, and you are one of them. You, too, are a tree that stands tall because YOU ARE THE LEGACY: A GENERATIONAL TREE.

YOU ARE THE LEGACY: A GENERATIONAL TREE is an adult allegory of our life experiences as seen through the growth process of a tree and the season or seasons they endure. The journey of our lives—and it is a journey—takes us from one season of our lives to another season. Many times these seasons leave us overwhelmed, depleted, and exhausted. We might even become depressed. These new seasons challenge us to grow. These new seasons challenge our belief system. These new seasons disrupt our lives. These new seasons disrupt our plans. Lastly, these new seasons cause character building.

YOU ARE THE LEGACY: A GENERATIONAL TREE is about a tree whose name is

"Young Tree" in the beginning but later gets the name "LEGACY." He is green and is very immature. He's selfish and asks question after question many times before he gives Old Tree, whose real name is "SACRIFICE," a chance to answer him. He will learn many lessons in this new world he finds himself in.

It is my hope as you read *YOU ARE THE LEGACY: A GENERATIONAL TREE* you will come to see that in your own life, Old Tree, or Sacrifice, as I call him, has been giving you love, advice, direction, guidance, comfort, healing, help, friendship, salvation, deliverance, provision, and protection along the way. These are "Truth Seeds," which I hope we will pass on to the next generation. These are the "Seeds" that build "LEGACY." YOU ARE THE LEGACY: A GENERATIONAL TREE!

So, let's all plant seeds for the next generation. Not just the seeds that will produce visible trees, but the seeds that only the heart can see. YOU ARE THE LEGACY: A GENERATIONAL TREE. This is the purpose of this book.

Womb Of The Earth

Plop, plop, plop went the last drops of rain as they fell from the limb of an ageless old tree onto the leaves of a scrawny green sapling like water dripping down from a water spout. Although the drops annoyed him, those drops also awakened him to a life of hope. The moistened ground allowed him to push past the darkness of despair. It allowed him to push himself through the many layers of dirt that once smothered him. Somehow that one last drop of rain refreshed him, restored him and it makes him feel empowered.

The Reaction To The Light

The previous world had surrounded him with darkness and smothered him with hopelessness. He felt helpless, useless, worthless and he saw no reason for his existence. Now, the young tree is in the presence of a shimmering light. Had that light not appeared when it did, the young tree would have had to face massive thunderstorms, disastrous winds and a different kind of darkness unknown to him in this new world also. He has been spared them for the moment the rain has disappeared and the winds have subsided. He has light, though it is unfamiliar to him and he has to adjust to it like one does without shade.

He gladly welcomes the warmth that comes from the light that shines between the ageless old tree limbs as he gazes upward. The light causes the young tree to experience the exhibit of hues that encircle him like an artist who carefully knew where to place each stroke. The air smells like sweet perfume. Even though he can't name the things that are producing the sweet smell that's coming from the roses, lilacs and honey suckles as they dance around him, he does however appreciate them. The other world smells rancid. It smells like mold. It smells of rottenness: like the smell of sulfur, rotten eggs and decaying plants. The smell in the other world is worse than the smell of a skunk.

Exceptional Differences

He is, however, startled by the old tree, but, the old tree hasn't meant to startle the sapling. He has only positioned himself there so he can protect the young tree. The old tree is taking in consideration the brightness of the light. He understands experiencing too much light too soon is just as damaging as not having enough light.

Young tree notices the old tree and their similarities. He notices they each have leaves. He notices they each have branches and they each have trunks. It isn't the old tree's trunk nor is it the way the old tree waves his branches that causes the sapling concern. Oh no! This old tree moves his branches gracefully in the air like clouds floating across the sky, like a dove spreading its wings for flight. It certainly isn't anything the old tree is saying to the young sapling because there haven't been any exchange of words yet. What will their conversations be since the young tree is so startled? Who are you? What is your name? How did you get here and have you been here very long? Did you experience any hardships in the other world? Assuming the Old Tree must have come from the other world.

Yet there can be no answers because there have been no verbal questions, only those questions in the young tree's mind. So the things that are really noticeable and something that can't be ignored were their differences. Old Tree is tall, but not just tall.

Amazingly Tall!
Exceptionally Tall!
Remarkably Tall!
Strikingly Tall!

Old tree is tall enough to pick a star from the sky. In fact, old tree is tall enough to have placed the stars there in the beginning of time. It is these noticeable differences that makes Young Tree question himself. "Why am I so tiny and this old tree so towering? Why am I so puny and this old tree so strong? Will l ever be worthy of attention like this old tree?"

Yet there is something about being in the presence of the old tree that makes the sapling feel secure. The old tree's stance is mighty powerful in appearance like he's a great warrior; although everything around him appears to be calm and peaceful. Everything seems to be in harmony with this old tree. Old tree seems to bring order to everything that exists in this new world. There doesn't appear to be any chaos in this new world. This world is peaceful and tranquil. Young tree thinks to himself that maybe this ageless old tree will be the key to his own survival in this new world. This world of light.

The Reward of Support

He doesn't know why he took up residence in the old world. It wouldn't have been his choice. It was dreadful. Now he has to figure out why he's in this new world. What is his purpose in this new world? What is his assignment in this new world? Will this be a temporary or a permanent arrangement? Will this world be dreadful also? His only hope and perhaps his only reward for journeying to this new world is that he might get to know the old tree. He's hoping the old tree beside him will become his friend. He has none in that other world and there is no way the young tree wants to go through this new world alone without someone to talk to. Plus, having someone provide him with a little moral support will also be to his advantage, something that was missing in the old world.

The Daily Struggles

In the other world, each plant saw itself as having the right to do whatever it wanted to for survival. Young tree had been devastated and terrified of the old world. He hadn't received any physical, mental, emotional, or spiritual support. In the old world, his delicate little roots would spread in so many different directions, becoming entangled, causing him great pain with each movement upward. In fact, some of his roots had grown so wild that in an attempt to stabilize himself, his roots grabbed onto rocks, wrapping themselves tighter and tighter around them as to refuse to let go. While other roots couldn't stand the pressures and tension, they pulled away. Many of these roots pushed and pulled against one another, trying to make themselves comfortable wherever they could. When they couldn't make themselves comfortable, they just broke off from the rest of his body. Some of his roots at times were so greedy they took in more minerals, nutrients, and water than his little pale body could absorb. No, accepting new roots wasn't going to come easy.

Exhaustion Impedes The Vision

Now, the bright light glowing between the Old Tree's branches as he moves them is so bright, it alters the sapling's vision making it impossible for him to see why this new world has so much more to offer him. The beauty of this new world alone is worth choosing because of the colors, and the many creations not seen in the previous world. The calm atmosphere alone is worth choosing to be in this new world. There's no chaos. There is an abundance of love, affection and appreciate for the things in this new world. True light is available to all who want it in this new world.

However, the young tree is too exhausted, a result of the previous world of darkness, to truly appreciate all the light can bring to him. He wants to escape. He wants to get away from the light. But where can he go? He can't possibly return back to the other world; it would be worse than facing what may or may not lie ahead in this present world. He can't possibly return to the stench he just left. So he'll just have to embrace this new world's challenges. He will have to face the new unknowns. Old tree's longevity might just be what young tree needs to convince him he can make it in this new world of uncertainties.

If the young tree can just get some rest, he can then gather enough courage to introduce himself to the old tree and get some answers about this new world. Right now, the sapling just needs rest. He will get answers later and that will be soon enough.

Maturity Comes with a Price, It Stands Alone

No other tree can really ever compare to this tree. True, the old tree is taller than all the other trees, but there are other reasons why the old tree stands above the others. Other trees displayed signs of weakness. Their limbs falling and breaking without any reason. His branches however seem to embrace the world like a mother swaddling her baby. While other trees' leaves faded and crumbled with any sign of a challenge, old tree's leaves seem to form the shape of a crown, signifying he has authority. While other trees were puny, Old Tree is a pillar of strength and no doubt unmovable, unless of course he wants to be moved. All these features demonstrate he has endurance. They demonstrate his maturity. These are things Young Tree will have to develop. Before the Young Tree can reach a certain level of maturity, he will have to experience more dirt, face more storms, and more floods. Perhaps, Young Tree will even face mudslides. He will also be confronted with discouraging winds, barrenness, and more loneliness. The severity of the heat and continuous pressures of daily living will overwhelm him.

If he thought he wanted to give up before, he certainly will want to when he has to encounter an enemy called:

Fear!
Doubt!
Unbelief!
Regret!
Failure!

Each of these enemies will try introducing him to the "ION" family and these enemies will influence choices. This will result in:

Addiction!

Confusion!

Disillusion!

Oppression!

Depression!

Isolation!

Separation!

Deception!

Temptation!

Still these enemies will try to get him acquainted with the "MENT" family.

Attachment!
Discouragement!
Resentment!
Disappointment!

Yet Young Tree can make it in this new world if he learns two important things: one the art of listening without interrupting and two the art of using self-control when tempted with new challenges. However, the young tree is too easily excitable to be patient. He wants nothing to do with waiting. He wants no delays. Because it's his young nature, Young Tree will ask question after question and many times before Old Tree has had the opportunity to answer the first one, which shows how immature the young tree really is. Yet, there's much to be gained through the Old Tree's answers and equally as much to be gained through the Old Tree's conduct.

The Salutation

Old tree waves one of his branches and scents of lilacs and roses awaken the young tree, and now he is ready to enjoy the splendor of this new world to its fullest. No longer pale from the other world that had robbed him of his colors, now his true colors are being showcased for all creation to see.

Green!

Green but not lush yet!

Somehow having his true colors unveiled gives him a renewed strength and for now his only objective is to learn about the extremely tall tree next to him. Young tree wants to know his name, and, besides, the old tree's features and his size have distinguished him already from the other trees; shouldn't his name, thinks the young tree.

"Goooood morning," he said, while elevating his voice making sure those around him know he is the one speaking. No one paid the young sapling any attention, except the old tree and that was because the old tree paid attention to everyone and everything. It is his responsibility to do so and the old tree is especially tenderhearted toward the younger saplings.

The old tree echoes back at the sapling the very same words, but with a voice less threatening much like that of a lamb rather than a lion, "Goooood Morning." "What's your name? Spoke the words from the delicate young sapling. "My name is SACRIFICE," replied the old tree.

As SACRIFICE says his name, a dove flies by and everything in the land feels a cool refreshing gentle breeze. "You don't have to call me SACRIFICE right now you can call me, 'Old Tree.'"

Sac-ri-fice is a most unusual name Young Tree thinks of himself as he continues to try to pronounce it. Whoever heard a name like Sac-ri-fice before, as he attempts to pronounce it again. What does it mean? The young tree certainly doesn't know. In the other world there were names like Bitterness, Captivity, Bondage, Stubbornness, and Unforgiving. In the other world there were names like Steal, Killer, Destroyer, and Hate. Although saying "Old Tree" seems a little outdated, Young Tree thinks it is still much easier to say than the name "SACRIFICE," although he is finally able to pronounce it. But not only that, the name "SACRIFICE" sounded too detached, too impersonal and scary. It sounded like a name from the other world and he doesn't want any other reminders from that old world.

"Old Tree," the young tree says while paying no attention to the dove that is accompanying the Old Tree nor the gentle breeze. "Don't you want to know my name?" The Old Tree spoke slowly. He spoke softly, "I already know your name."

Incredible thinks of the Young Tree, I haven't even told him my name yet, and he already knows it.

"How do you know my name? I haven't even told you," replied the young tree with a perplexed look on his face as if he just took a bite of a lemon from the garden he found himself in. Then he raised a few of his tender branches in the air as if to measure his against Old Tree's. Of course, there is no comparison. Old Tree's branches when raised into the air reminds you of a menorah letting in flickering light.

Old Tree smiles and declares, "I know everything, even your new name which you will receive in time."

The young tree thinks for a moment, well he does look like he's been around for a long time, maybe he does know everything. Then it occurred to the young tree I'm getting a new name. He is so excited he is getting a new name. He starts raising and waving his branches in celebration of his new name. He wonders what his new name will be. He wonders if he will like his new name. He wants to spin around, but he's immobile.

"Old Tree, what's my new name?" The young tree questioned.

Old Tree's response to the young tree is, "Let's not worry about your new name, let's just focus on your present name, which is 'Young Tree.'"

Young Tree feels he is being ignored when Old Tree doesn't announce his new name. Of course, Young Tree doesn't like that because the other world did that to him too many times.

They constantly ignored him. Old Tree never ignores. He just has his own timing for responding to one's questions. And so it will be with Young Tree; he won't get an answer before his time. That's part of Old Tree's plan.

Since Old Tree isn't responding to this question, another thought sparks a question from the curious young tree.

"Old Tree, how long have you been around?" Old Tree smiles and responds, "I've come through forty-two generations. You see, I AM before the beginning and I AM beyond the end."

"The beginning and ending of what?" Young Tree asks. Old Tree responds, "I am the beginning of all things and the ending of all things." And this is Old Tree's only explanation.

It's confusing, Young Tree thinks to himself, "How can he be the beginning of all things and at the same time the ending of all things?" Thinking none of this makes sense to him, he made a decision to just ponder over it.

Young Tree will learn many lessons in this new world including how Old Tree is the beginning of all things and the ending of all things. Young Tree will learn his purpose. He will learn his destiny. He will learn endurance. He will learn pain and more suffering. He will learn what happens when you have enemies. He will learn love and forgiveness. And the greatest thing Young Tree will learn is the connection between him and Old Tree.

An Awareness

Throughout the day, Young Tree watches things move around the Old Tree like flowers with wings. Young Tree sees things with red and black spots, and he sees things with black and yellow bodies and they too fly. He notices morning glories, for-get-me-nots, lilies, sweet peas, and tulips displaying their colors of purple, pinks, oranges, greens, and yellows. He sees vines that aren't entangled like those of the other world. He sees reds, yellows, blues, and other shades like those seen in a rainbow.

He sees things that fly like doves, eagles, and hummingbirds. He sees things that move rather quickly like cheetahs, jaguars, lions, and tigers. Then he sees things that move unhurried like turtles, snails, and koalas. He sees jumping things like frogs, kangaroos, and rabbits.

He sees creatures coming and going, but he is perplexed that he seems to be the only thing that isn't moving. His leaves move. His branches move, but that of course is all. He doesn't move. He isn't going anywhere. Perhaps he's even stuck. He fails to realize he isn't the only thing that can't move or that is stationary, which proves again just how green the Young Tree is.

The Purpose Behind a Move

"Old Tree," called Young Tree, and before Old Tree can answer, Young Tree blurts the question, "Why can't I move?" And then Young Tree adds, "I see more things moving in this new world than were in the old world. I see things moving all around you for your enjoyment."

"Well, Young Tree, some things can move, but other things have to stay rooted and grounded if they're going to survive the seasons that lie ahead," states Old Tree. "Moreover, Young Tree, if you are moved, it's because someone has chosen to plant you somewhere else," and then Old Tree added, "If you are moved it is because something with extraordinary power does it. "Young Tree, if you are moved, there's a purpose behind the move," commented Old Tree. "Young Tree if you are moved, it is because you have an assignment to complete." Young Tree realized Old Tree used the word "you" instead of using the word "we." Young Tree thinks to himself, "Why doesn't Old Tree use the word 'we'? After all, aren't we the same except for the Old Tree's height and stature? Aren't our purposes the same to enjoy this new world? Aren't our assignments the same to showcase our beauty in this new world so others can see just how specular we are?"

But Old Tree reminds Young Tree, "Remember, Young Tree, the belief systems in this new world, though not like the belief systems of the old world, will still try tossing you to and fro. Young Tree, deceptive winds will try tossing you to and fro as well." There are some things about Young Tree that will need to remain immovable at least for now.

Young Tree can't imagine anyone or anything strong enough to move Old Tree. He understands other things being moved, but he can't imagine Old Tree being moved under any circumstances. So Young Tree disregarded the statement that Old Tree made just like young ones do whenever they don't want to hear something contrary to their thinking or their own beliefs. Besides, Young Tree feels safe, secure, and no longer feels intimidated by Old Tree's stature. One thing is for sure: Old Tree makes Young Tree feel alive.

Wrong Assumptions

For a moment, he makes the assumption what it would be like to not have the Old Tree around. He came to a rapid conclusion, that perhaps he wouldn't be safe or secure in this new world after all. He wouldn't have the protection of Old Tree, and he wouldn't come to know Old Tree's love. Something he felt the first moment Old Tree spoke to him, although he couldn't explain it. Young Tree isn't aware that his rich heritage comes through Old Tree. And he isn't aware that his inheritance will also come through the Old Tree. The only thing he understands is he doesn't feel abandoned with the Old Tree around. His not feeling abandoned makes him make this bold statement. "I'll never be moved, no matter what happens to me," said Young Tree. He is only trying to convince himself, reassure himself that nothing is capable of moving him, especially with Old Tree around to defend him.

Denial

Once Young Tree raised all his branches, Young Tree saw an abundance of other trees. And he realizes he hasn't been the only tree that has had to fight to free itself to get to this new world. There were others. Yet, some of these same trees close to Young Tree are being cut down. They are being cut down because they have shown no sign of life, with leaves drying up and crumbling to the earth, branches so brittle and breaking with the slightest movement or touch. It is obvious these trees aren't fruitful trees and haven't been from their beginning. They received their water from a polluted stream, and more importantly they are causing other trees to become polluted and contaminated. It's the worst thing that can happen to any tree. Yes, they have to be cut down. They just refuse to let go of things from the other world.

Although Young Tree knows some trees have to be cut down, he is confused at the sight of seeing trees near him being cut down. His thoughts are if he is in close proximity to the Old Tree and so are some of the other trees close to him, then why would they be cut down. Young Tree shouted, in disbelief, "Old Tree look over there, they're cutting down yet another one of us!"

Old Tree moves one of his branches slightly, allowing the sun to beam down upon Young Tree and to take Young Tree's focus away from other trees being cut down. He knew Young Tree might start panicking and stressing whether or not he might be the next tree to be cut down. He knew he had to avert Young Tree's focus from worrying about things he doesn't have control over.

Surface Roots

Short on patience, a disgusted Young Tree complained, "Why is it so bright?" "Why is it so hot?" "Can somebody shut this thing off?" Young Tree looked around hoping to find some relief from the heat and then saw a reflection of himself. "I can see myself in the water, Old Tree."

"Young Tree, that's called a reflection," said Old Tree. "Reflections are good, if they reflect the right images. If it reflects good and not evil," replied Old Tree. "Young Tree, the seasons are changing again, but if your roots are continuously refreshed by the river that flows through me you can make it through any season," commented Old Tree.

"A river runs through the Old Tree. How can that be?" says Young Tree to himself.

It seems Young Tree has a reservoir of questions. He wants to ask about the river inside the Old Tree but he is still trying to understand how his roots work, since it was his roots that caused him the most trouble in the other world.

"Will my roots reach that far?" asked Young Tree.

"Yes, and they will carry you a long way," answered the Old Tree, "even up a hill."

"So, it's important that my roots are entwined and woven with yours?" asked Young Tree. "Yes, Young Tree, it's very important," replied Old Tree.

Old Tree's roots were exceptionally long, each one traveling to other trees like mazes across the land. Yet, Old Tree's roots never once became entangled like Young Tree had before he surfaced to this new world.

Young Tree gives a long sigh and utters the

words, "I AM SO HOT." "I WISH THE SUN, WOULD JUST GO AWAY AND HIDE."

Old Tree speaks to Young Tree about his complaints against the brightness of the sun and the scorching heat. "Young Tree, stopping the sun from shining will put you back in total darkness. Young Tree, if you return to utter darkness again it will stunt your growth forever.

Remember you have to learn to adjust to change."

The Cost of a Hill

Young Tree notices a very tall, staggered hill in the distance. It's this staggered hill that is about to bring about changes in both of their lives. These changes are coming sooner than Young Tree realizes and these changes won't come without sacrifices on both their parts.

"Old Tree, I would love to be able to move so I can climb those hills over there. Then I would be able to see things from high up just like you," voiced Young Tree. "I am tired of looking at things from down here. It's getting boring," commented Young Tree.

"I'm sure you would, Young Tree, but if you had to carry a heavy load up one, you might not want to climb it," stated Old Tree. "It might just be too costly for you," he added. The Old Tree is always trying to get the Young Tree to see that everything comes with a SACRIFICE. Old Tree wants Young Tree to climb higher, not a hill or mountain seen with natural eyes, but climb a mountain with eyes that see from the heart.

However, that isn't likely to happen today. It's too hot and too muggy. It's so hot a few of Young Tree's leaves are scorched. A few of them are wilted. Even a couple of his branches are splintering. Right now, he disapproves of the heat. He disapproves of the high temperatures and he certainly disapproves of the sun. Since Young Tree disapproves of all these things, he is simply more irritable than usual. All because he has no control over it or anything. But he does have control over some things he just doesn't know yet. He welcomes rain, even a few drops to satisfy him, but there's no rain in sight. He complains about the sun again. He even complains to the sun in hopes that the sun might go hide somewhere, anywhere, just as long as he can get some relief. The sun, however, pays no attention to Young Tree. It gets its orders from a greater light.

Yet the sun isn't Young Tree's problem, at least not the s-u-n. Dying from thirst or so he thinks Young Tree cries, "How can one possibly make it through this hot weather?"

"SING," said Old Tree. "Make it personable!"

Make It Personable, "SING"

Young Tree thinks he heard Old Tree say, sing. "Sing?" Giggled Young Tree, then he questioned whether he had the ability to do so. "I can do that Old Tree?" asked the curious Young Tree. "I can sing," he says with more emphasis.

Enthusiasm in his voice Old Tree said, "Yes, Sing," "Young Tree. "Sing joyful noises," as he swings his branches in the air freely. "I love to hear singing." "Singing makes me happy!" "It brings peace in confusion! It brings harmony in chaos! "You'll see it will make you happy and then you'll want to celebrate the changing of the seasons rather than whining and complaining about them." "So, Sing, Young Tree, Sing."

Then Old Tree added something else. "Singing even makes dead things fall off you, but don't worry yourself with that Young Tree, time takes care of everything," voiced Old Tree.

This brought another question to Young Tree's mind.

"How do I sing?" "What do I sing?" Inquired Young Tree.

"Well," explained Old Tree, "You really don't sing, you just hum in the wind and the wind is what really makes the melody and the music."

"What's wind, Old Tree?" Asked Young Tree, who is eager to learn this lesson. "Young Tree, the wind is an invisible force with dynamic power. You can't see it; you just feel its effects as it moves things—" However, before Old Tree could say the word "around" Young Tree shouted, "Can the wind move you?"

"Yes," answered Old Tree, "it can, and when it does it sets you on the path called purpose. It sets you on a directional course." Old Tree has always known his purpose for being in the earth, he was just trying to help Young Tree find his purpose.

Perceiving Young Tree's thoughts, Old Tree just smiles and extends his branches upward to the sky protecting Young Tree from the sun. He knows Young Tree has learned several lessons that day, now he wants Young Tree to rest. They will talk later. So Young Tree finishes his day with Old Tree singing him a song, a love song.

Shaking and Shifting from the Inside

A new day has dawned. Young Tree is still resting when the sudden clamoring and commotion has awakened him. Young Tree feels the ground move under him with each thumping sound. He tries holding on, but his roots are losing their grip. How could he possibly keep from losing his leaves with the shaking taking place? He isn't prepared for this new challenge. He thinks to himself, he might not be ready for this new world after all.

"What's happening?" "What's going on?" "Everything inside me is shaking and shifting." "Am I being uprooted, Old Tree?"

"Hold steady my young friend, you're not going anywhere. As I told you before, you'll be here from one generation to another to declare my works, Young Tree. Even if you were to be moved, you're not going to move yet. You have more lessons to learn about life. You need this season and the new season ahead. Young Tree, hold steady and dig your roots deeper. They'll help you stand, and standing will help you endure," proclaimed Old Tree.

Young Tree gripes, "that's all I seem to be doing, enduring and for what."

Not only can Young Tree feel strange things happening under him. He can hear strange and evil sounds coming from beneath him as well. But not only can he hear them from, beneath him, he can also hear them coming from within. He hears the words, "you are never going to make it in this new world." He hears words like "you are a failure." Then he hears words like, "nobody wants you in that new world." "You should just go back to where you came from." "You deserted them, anyway." The voices just kept coming. He tried shaking them off but they wouldn't leave. He was scared because he didn't know how to handle the voices. And the voices just kept getting louder inside him or so it appeared they were. And that's not all that is strange; now strange things are being tossed right in his direction.

"Hey, watch it, you're throwing dirt on me!"

No one paid any attention to him. After all, he's just another young sapling. Dirt had been thrown at Young Tree before so that was really anything new. What made it new this time was the dirt included stones and the stones hurt more than the dirt. "THAT HURTS," he said when one of the stones hit his trunk. Young Tree had things touch his leaves and branches before, but this time it wasn't touching — no, not touching — but attacking the main part of his support system. It was attacking the frame of his body. "STOP HITTING ME WITH

THOSE STONES!"

One of the stones had "traitor" written on it, another stone had "backstabber," and one of the stones said "hypocrite," all because Young Tree left the other world.

"THAT REALLY HURTS!" screamed Young Tree.

He is mad, no, not mad, but angry. He is so angry in desperation to get away, he tries moving his trunk but he can't move anything other than his branches. "If I could just move somewhere else," he says to himself. Young Tree can't figure out why this is happening to him. He hollered, "I MEAN IT! STOP HITTING ME! STOP HITTING ME RIGHT NOW! STOP DOING THAT! YOU'RE MAKING ME MAD, REALLY MAD! I KEEP TELLING YOU THAT HURTS! YOU BETTER STOP THROWING STONES AT ME BEFORE OLD TREE DOES

SOMETHING TO YOU!" Suddenly the throwing of stones stopped the same way they started: without notice. Young Tree is so relieved and gets so excited he says to himself, "I knew Old Tree would come through for me if I complained loud enough."

Old Tree isn't moved by Young Tree's complaining. If anything, all Young Tree's complaining did was open the door for more new lessons to be learned, but this time they will be self-inflicted. Yes, this season will truly be a testing of Young Tree's faith.

Broken Promises

Right then, a long object hit one of his tender branches. The blow causes one of Young Tree's branches to crack from the inside. This blow causes part of his limbs to break open causing infection to form. Although he is hurting and although he is in pain, he is more disappointed and frustrated that Old Tree, his friend, his best friend, his brother, or so he thought, hasn't come to his rescue. After all, Old Tree promised, Old Tree vowed he would always be there for him. Old Tree promised he would never leave him. He promises he will always hear his cries. He even vowed he will always take care of him and protect him, but Young Tree is now asking, "Where is the protection he promised me?" "How come I don't feel safe?" Young Tree needed that protection right now, or so he thought.

Is his protection asleep? Is his protection hiding, or does he just not care anymore? For whatever reason Old Tree isn't answering. "Old Tree I'm in so much pain," Young Tree states.

Old Tree isn't answering because silence is as much of an answer as talking or speaking. However, Young Tree's newest lesson is to learn that Old Tree is trying to get him to understand he has to believe in himself. To believe he can make it without grumbling and complaining. To believe he can make it without always protesting when things don't go his way. The Old Tree is building confidence.

Since Young Tree still lacks the confidence in himself and Old Tree knows Young Tree will remain barren until he matures, then and only then will he be able to bear fruit that remains. If Young Tree can just trust the wisdom Old Tree possesses, he can then trust that Old Tree will never lead him astray. He can understand Old Tree loves him, really loves him unconditionally. The wind carries a leaf from Old Tree, drops it on Young Tree and the healing process starts once again. Then Young Tree falls asleep.

The Mudslinging Enemy

As if the banging, clanging, and thumping hasn't been enough, now water is flowing right in the direction of Young Tree. NO! It's sliding in his direction, an indication that things are really shifting! The water is so thick it is pushing everything in its path out of the way, leaving a mess on everything it touches, even Young Tree.

Young Tree fears for his life. He isn't sure what this new stuff is, but he knows it has the power to move him, because he saw other things larger than himself being moved. Although he himself is quite tall he is nowhere close to being the size of Old Tree. The removal of many trees is taking place in this move. Young Tree fears for his own life, too. He knows it has the power to change his course in life. His biggest fear is that it has the power to separate him from the Old Tree forever.

Baffled by everything happening and especially the thick substance that seems to have surrounded him, Young Tree cries, "What's this stuff?"

It has taken Young Tree a while to grab hold of Old Tree's roots, but he has finally done it.

"It's a mudslide, Young Tree," Old Tree told him.

Young Tree can no longer see Old Tree, but he thinks he can hear him faintly. The thick water bruised Young Tree severely, both physically and emotionally. His leaves fall from him like tear drops. Immediately, Young Tree starts to blame himself. "It's my fault. I should have stayed where I was." "I should have known this would happen."

He questions himself. "What have I done wrong?" "What am I doing wrong?" Thinking he had brought it on himself, he moves a few of his branches in hopes of getting away from the thick dirty water that is continuing to come toward him.

"Why?" he said in distress.

"Why do I have to go through this?"

"Why do I have to continue to struggle in this new world?" "Why does it feel dark again?" said Young Tree in anguish.

"Why do I feel the presence of evil like it's trying to attach itself to me?" Young Tree asked himself. Then he added, "I thought I was going to have peace in this new world before he let out a holler. "HELP!"

Young Tree is not about to get any peace now, not since the "ION" family showed up: Confusion, Disillusion, Oppression, Depression, Isolation, Loneliness, Separation, Deception and Temptation. There will be no sign of freedom if this family evil has their way. Their assignment is to keep Young Tree in a certain state of mind until he wants to destroy himself. However, Old Tree isn't going to let that happen.

Although there aren't any answers to his questions because somewhere right in the middle of the mudslide, Old Tree had stopped talking. Young Tree is fussing so much he can't hear Old Tree, anyway. So Old Tree's only response isn't really a verbal response at all. Old Tree just watches him from afar. He is waiting patiently for Young Tree to just settle down before he speaks again. Before Young Tree says something, Young Tree will wish he has never said. Young Tree thinks his discontentment is with Old Tree, but it's really with himself. For now, Young Tree will have to settle for the leaf the wind brought him from Old Tree's branch.

Young Tree looks terrible. He is covered in mud that's been slung on him and it will take days, weeks, maybe months before Young Tree will look or feel clean again. Old Tree is embarrassed, not for himself, but for Young Tree.

The Obvious Observation

Once Young Tree calms down, it suddenly occurs to him Old Tree has dirt and mud on him too, but he isn't allowing the dirt to bother him. Of course, Young Tree doesn't understand why Old Tree has dirt on him, anyway. Old Tree never says anything wrong. He never does anything wrong. He never gives a contrary look. More importantly, Old Tree doesn't seem the least bit concerned by the filth thrown at him or them. The Old Tree is always calm. He always has a peaceful countenance. It's as though the peace Old Tree has comes from within him. Old Tree has no frowns, nor any disturbing looks. He is not gloomy. Old Tree is always in control of his emotions. He's always in control of his feelings. Old Tree doesn't seem the least bit concerned by the filth thrown at him or them.

Young Tree doesn't realize that if you don't say anything when dirt is being thrown at you and you don't let the mudslinging get you down, it will eventually stop. Young Tree has to face the fact that he needs the kind of peace Old Tree carries.

Corrective Vision by a Touch

Young Tree is surprised to see Old Tree standing right there beside him where he has always been. However, Young Tree hasn't noticed because Young Tree has a habit of letting things cloud his mind. He has a way of not seeing the truth when the truth is right before his eyes.

Seeing the Old Tree, he sputters the words, "W---H---Y were they throwing dirt on me?" "Now, I'm filthy." "Old Tree, I stink!" "I reek worse than when I was in the other world." Old Tree started to laugh at Young Tree, because he did look funny and yes, he did indeed stink. Old Tree laughs because he knows Young Tree will try to cleanse himself, something impossible. Old Tree knows in order for Young Tree to get a proper cleansing, he will need fresh water that only comes from above. Old Tree knows all Young

Tree needs a touch of his love to reign down over him and he will be clean again.

The Touch of the Wind

Old Tree swings his enormous branches in the air, and a few leaves fall from them. As each leaf falls, it brings healing to whatever it touches, including Young Tree. Then Young Tree sees something else he hasn't seen before: whenever Old Tree swings his broad branches, things start moving. He thinks to himself, Old Tree must have something to do with the wind too, but he isn't sure how or what. He still can't understand why Old Tree is laughing at him. What can be so funny? he says to himself. "What have I done now to bring on such laughter? Besides, this isn't the time to be laughing," reasons the Young Tree.

Old Tree just smiles and says, "Young Tree, you think everything is always about you and what you want." "But Young Tree it's not always about you or what you want, in fact, most of the time it's about others and that's a lesson you will soon learn, the lesson of sacrificing yourself for another."

"Sacrificing," Young Tree thinks to himself, hmm that's part of Old Tree's name, he's mentioned that before. I just don't know what the name "SACRIFICE" has to do with me, he boldly proclaims." "Besides, I don't want to make any sacrifices. I like things just the way they are." Then he remembered Old Tree promised him a new name. "I wonder what my new name is going to be and when will I get this new name," another thing Young Tree wants to know. Young Tree is learning so many new things, so many new lessons he can't even keep up with the seasons. Young Tree believes that Old Tree's ability to provide safety for his own personal enjoyment, his own personal needs is Young Tree's only concern for now.

Just then a dove flew between Old Tree's branches and an overwhelming peace came upon the land. It reminds Young Tree one more time how important it is to have a personal relationship with Old Tree, because everything that touches Old Tree becomes serene.

All nature!

All creation!

The wind blows gently and Young Tree thinks he hears the wind singing. The wind seems to be singing yet another word Young Tree hasn't heard before, and it certainly is another word he can't pronounce. The wind keeps repeating the sound until Young Tree is able to slowly pronounce each syllable, though it takes Young Tree some time to do so.

    H A L

        L E

            LU

                J A H!

When the syllables are put together, he hears the word, HALLELUJAH, and just hearing the word echoing throughout the land causes Young Tree to leap inside with joy. Unspeakable joy! Unexplainable Joy! This single word brought peace to this troubled, and confused sapling. Young Tree feels at peace with himself and with the others. He has never experienced peace like this before, not in the previous world nor in this new world until now. He feels so alive. So revived.

Maybe the peace Young Tree is feeling is because he's finally learning to trust, have confidence in, and rely on the things Old Tree is saying. Perhaps the peace Young Tree is feeling is because he is learning to surrender his will over to Old Tree. Yet, Young Tree is puzzled why Old Tree has the name that he does. If Young Tree had his way, he would have given Old Tree the name HALLELUJAH instead of SACRIFICE from the beginning. Young Tree believes Old Tree should have a much more exciting name than SACRIFICE.

Now Young Tree is learning to ask for what he needs, not just the things he wants so he asks Old Tree to give him some more shade. He doesn't have enough shade covering him and he thinks this is the reason he is so hot.

"Old Tree," commented Young Tree.

"Yes, Young Tree," answered the Old Tree.

"It's so hot and the light is much brighter than it was when I first entered into the new world. Can I have some shade please?" asked the Young Tree. Then he started to say the word want, but then changed it to, "I need to get away from, I'm trying to sing," states Young Tree.

"Well," said Old Tree, "If the true light isn't shining upon you, you can't see things clearly and you can't appreciate this new world. In fact, you can't sing with accuracy without true light." Once again, Young Tree isn't paying attention to Old Tree. He is so absorbed with the sound of his own voice he isn't able to recall the song the wind just sang. It's as if he's praising himself instead of the Old Tree.

The Protest

Young Tree barely makes it through one season before it's time for him to go on to something else. To learn more unpleasant lessons.

"How can I learn anything or retain anything if the wind keeps changing?" "I will never be able to master the seasons of life," thinks Young Tree. The "MENT" family: Discouragement! Resentment! Torment! Abandonment! has him thinking only of himself and Young Tree is depressed. Somewhere between the changing of the seasons, he has forgotten to sing and is focusing only on himself using the word "I" in every sentence he announces.

Young Tree says in desperation, "Old Tree, I'VE HAD IT AND I CAN'T TAKE IT ANYMORE."
"I'M TRYING TO OBEY YOU."
"I'M TRYING OLD TREE TO PLEASE YOU."

Then Young Tree says, I'M ABOUT TO … But Old Tree stops him and won't let him finish. Old Tree doesn't want to hear one more "I" because he knows all Young Tree needs to do is just be grateful for where he is, how far he has come and what he has.

"What do you mean, you can't take it anymore?" said Old Tree. "Young Tree, the seasons are changing again. When the seasons change it means the seasons of your life are changing too. Young tree you can never be greater than the one who created you, stated Old Tree."

"The seasons change so quickly, Old Tree," "I can never figure out what season I'm in," said Young Tree. One moment it's raining and we have mudslides, next it's hot and I start to wither. Then I get down and I feel alone. I just can't take it anymore. The weight of it all is just too much.

"Young Tree," said Old Tree, "No cross, no crown and every tree will have their own cross to carry, even you."

"What's a cross?" "What's a crown?" asked Young Tree.

Old Tree gives Young Tree just enough information to keep Young Tree from worrying. "A cross are the trials and temptations you face daily and a crown is something you wear when you've overcome trials and temptations," said Old Tree.

"I've already had enough temptations and trials. I'm an expert at them now. There ought to be less trials and temptations now since I've learned how to deal with them, said Young Tree."

Old Tree waves a branch "What do you mean Young Tree?" Old Tree asked, already knowing what Young Tree's response would be.

"Remember the dirt they threw all over me and

remember all the mudslinging, when I certainly didn't deserve it and of course I hadn't done anything wrong. Well, I'm used to all that now," proclaimed Young Tree. "In fact, I don't really let it bother me now."

Once again the Old Tree just smiles. Young Tree has surely brought him great joy but, the lessons aren't over yet for Young Tree.

Cut Down to Size

"Old Tree, look they're cutting another tree down and it's so late in the day," said Young Tree.

"Yes, Young Tree the axe is laid to every root, which doesn't produce good fruit. Then it's cut down and thrown in the fire. There are only a few exceptions," declared Old Tree.

Young Tree said, "Old Tree I don't like the sound of that."

"Young Tree, I've told you before, all you have to do is stand and stop letting every little thing make you so miserable."

"But Old Tree I'm afraid of fire," said Young Tree, "I've seen what it's done to other trees."

"Young Tree you won't burn, just like you didn't drown when the flood waters came. Just stay rooted and grounded in me my little friend, and always listen to my voice," added Old Tree.

"How can I continue to stay rooted and grounded if I am constantly facing storms, dealing with trials, facing temptations, and being exposed to troubles?" asked Young Tree.

"Abide, dwell, and stay in my presence, Young Tree, I Am right here to comfort you," said Old Tree. "I'm here to protect you as well," stated Old Tree.

Clear drops of liquid fell from Young Tree's face as he whispered the words, "I love you Old Tree."

Old Tree tells Young Tree "I love you too, Legacy."

Young Tree hears the words, "I love you too," but he falls asleep after he hears these words and doesn't get to hear his new name.

Old Tree knows Young Tree has already experienced a multitude of lessons already. He also knows Young Tree has many more to learn. He knows these words will comfort him and he will get a good rest for the night.

The *I's* Have Finally Done It

Several days have passed when Young Tree says, "Guess what the other trees are saying about us?" "Guess what they are doing?" As if Old Tree didn't already know. "They're talking about how much time we spend together," said Young Tree. "You know what I think, Old Tree, I think they are jealous of me. I think they are afraid of all the attention I'm getting from you.

They are jealous about all the advice you are giving me. They are envious of our relationship." There are a lot of things Old Tree will excuse but pride isn't one of them. He knows pride always produces a fall. He doesn't want the Young Tree to fall like other trees have.

"Young Tree, this thinking is *pride*," Old Tree says in anger. "It knocked at the door of your thought life and now you aren't able to comprehend the truth." He continues, "This is so unnecessary when I love each tree that is created in my image." "This is so unnecessary when each tree is privileged to the same information." "This is so unnecessary when I devote my time to all my trees equally when they call on me." "I need you to understand, Young Tree, pride leads to selfishness and stubbornness." "Young Tree, when you are selfish and stubborn you aren't willing to listen to sound advice," says Old Tree. Then Old Tree added, "Young Tree right now you need sound advice, as he raised his voice like a roaring angry lion."

Pride is the one thing the Old Tree doesn't tolerate. He can accept one having confidence in themselves but he knows pride makes one think they are better than others. When one takes a ride with pride it will bring about a new season. In this new season the lessons Young Tree will learn will be more difficult than the previous seasons he has endured.

Young Tree ponders on the words of Old Tree and realizes he made Old Tree angry. But the question is, is Old Tree so angry that he won't sing a song to Young Tree, as he usually does?

"Old Tree," he asked, "Will you sing me a song?"

Even though Old Tree is angry, he will always let his love for Young Tree and the others shine through. So Old Tree does; he sings a love song.

The Weight of the Fight

Sleeping through the night, Young Tree's limbs glistened like white glitter was painted on them. When he awakens, he wants to say, "Good Morning, Old Tree" but it's a struggle for him and all he can say while shivering is "I'm c-o-o-o-l-d, so c-o-o-o-ld." Then as he looks around for Old Tree, he hears crackling. Some of the crackling is coming from him as he moves his limbs and some of the crackling is coming from other trees. Because of all the crackling, Young Tree feels naked. He's ashamed that his nakedness is being exposed for all the other trees to see, as if he were an exhibit in an art museum.

Young Tree is so lonely. "Why isn't the Old Tree around to cover me?" he thinks. "Something is really wrong this time," he adds to his thoughts. He can't handle the cold and he falls back asleep again.

When he awakens for the second time of the day, he tries moving one of his branches, but he is too stiff. Every part of him is frozen in place. He has never had an experience quite like this one before or at least he can't remember doing so. Straining his voice to be heard by Old Tree he asks for help.

"Old Tree, H-E-L-P! P-L-E-A-S-E, HELP ME" is Young Tree's cry in desperation. "I'm so cold. I'm scared." "I'm so scared, Old Tree."

Old Tree shook something from his branches and it fell gracefully onto Young Tree. Young Tree immediately feels better although it still feels much like a deep freezer for all the other trees. His chills are gone and of course the minute he starts feeling better, the wind starts moving things around again. Little white flakes from the sky fall like feathers falling out of a pillow. Then the feather-like flakes come together swirling and twirling so fast they cause a tornado blowing trash in the branches of Young Tree. Young Tree murmurs to himself, "I wish I was like Old Tree cause absolutely nothing seems to bother Old Tree."

NOT THE SUN!

NOT THE FLOOD-RAINS! NOT MUD!

NOT THE GUSHING WINDS!

NOT THE COLD!

NOT THE FLAKES THAT LOOK LIKE FEATHERS!

NOT EVEN OTHER TREES!

Young Tree complains and struggles with the wind. Before he had questions about the wind, now he is fighting the wind and one of his branches breaks off. Then another branch breaks off and Young Tree begins to panic. He thinks he might lose them all. He has never lost this many branches before. Never! Yet Young Tree still has more branches left than he realizes. This season is really frightening for Young Tree. Old Tree really wants to reach out to Young Tree, but he can't. Love is letting him be tested. Young Tree must endure this lesson by himself.

"Old Tree, Old Tree," "Where are you?" cried Young Tree. He can't see the Old Tree because of the things he has inflicted upon himself. Then in anguish he says, "I CAN'T SEE YOU!" "I CAN'T FEEL YOU!" "I NEED YOU!" "I NEED YOU, OLD TREE!" I'M GOING TO DIE IF YOU DON'T COME HELP ME! "I JUST CAN'T TAKE ANYMORE OF THIS!' "WHERE ARE YOU, OLD TREE?" "YOU PROMISED YOU WILL NEVER LEAVE ME.

YOU PROMISED TO NEVER FORSAKE ME." Every time Young Tree faces challenges, he thinks Old Tree has left him alone.

The weight of the white flakes is too much for Young Tree. Under the weight of the flakes, he feels hopeless again, and without warning another branch hits the ground. Young Tree cried, "I don't understand why you don't help me." Young Tree sheds more leaves that drop to the ground like tears. "Old Tree, you've always been here for me." Moaning he says, "The winds are not even singing," but what Young Tree really should be saying is he isn't singing. In one more last desperate cry Young Tree says, "How do I stop fighting the wind?" "How do I keep from breaking any more branches?" "I need my limbs and I need to be able to move them without them always breaking off." Finally, Old Tree speaks, "Sway with the wind." "Extend those branches and sway with the wind." However, Young Tree is too busy struggling and fighting with the wind to hear Old Tree's advice.

Again, he asks, "How do I stop fighting the wind, Old Tree?"

"Keep seeking me." "See me with your heart," is Old Tree's only reply. "What will that take, Old Tree?" Ask Young Tree.

"Young Tree, it will take your faith," declares Old Tree." "It will require believing." "This will require something I don't really think I possess right now," answered Young Tree in total frustration. Young Tree was getting tired of all Old Tree's challenges. "I'm wounded. Look at my scars! I'm still cold! My covering is still gone and I'm dying! I'm really dying! I'm about to give up my last breath!" Of course, Young Tree is exaggerating.

Celebratory Season

The next time words are exchanged between the two of them, the sky has opened up and so has Young Tree's heart. Young Tree has finally realized he has to surrender his will to the will of Old Tree. So Young Tree does something he has never done before. Young Tree bows *all* of his leaves to Old Tree and says, "Old Tree, I give up." "I surrender." At that very moment he surrenders he knows to call the Old Tree "SACRIFICE." Instantly and without delay, All Nature and All Creation join together in harmony and rejoice with singing. Singing that is heard wherever SACRIFICE'S leaves reach. Singing that is heard wherever SACRIFICE'S branches reach. Singing that is heard wherever SACRIFICE'S roots reach. Although Young Tree isn't aware of it, the rejoicing is really for and about him. Young Tree thinks it's because the sky opened for SACRIFICE. But it's because Young Tree confessed "I surrender." This is exactly what Old Tree has been waiting for before he could give Young Tree his new name. SACRIFICE quiets creation with the raising of his right branch and says, "I am before the beginning and beyond the end." Young Tree, it is time." This time Young Tree doesn't ask questions. Young Tree doesn't interrupt Old Tree. Young Tree doesn't boast of his own accomplishments. Young Tree has made the decision to just wait patiently for Old Tree to speak, no matter how long it takes. He has come to understand Old Tree's time is far better than him doing things in his own timing.

    Old Tree is so delighted to declare, "Young Tree, today your name is no longer Young Tree; that's your old name. It came with your old nature. From this day forward," as SACRIFICE proudly raises his branches and his leaves move in harmony with the wind" he says, "Today your new name is "LEGACY." When this happens, something else special happens on the inside of Legacy but it shows up on his outsides. Legacy blossoms with joy. His leaves are healthy, vibrant green, and growing at a rapid rate. On the side of the leaf that looks upward, it's olive in color, but on the side of the leaf that faces downward it's hunter green in color like a warrior. Now he's able to bear an abundance of fruit. Legacy is so grateful to have a new name, he extends his branches and he is able to touch other trees as this is a celebration within itself. This is a sign he is maturing. He is the happiest he has been in a long time, so happy he joins in the singing. He is more peaceful. He's exercising more patience. He is gentle, kind, and more respectful of others. His faith has grown, making him more cooperative to change. Lastly, Legacy is confident in himself.

The celebration for him continued for days, for weeks, and even months.

The Markings of Truth

Legacy calls for Old Tree, but there's no answer. Maybe it is because Legacy called him Old Tree rather SACRIFICE. Again, he calls for Old Tree but again there's no answer. Legacy has forgotten to call Old Tree by his new name. Then he remembers to say SACRIFICE and still there's no answer. Legacy looks around for SACRIFICE and when he finally locates SACRIFICE, he has rich plum color markings all over himself. It's the color one might associate with Kings and then he realizes these markings must mean death is coming soon for SACRIFICE. Other tree markings were pale in color like strawberries when they were cut down. They only had a couple of markings. SACRIFICE, however, has at least twenty nine or more stripes. Legacy really understands just how special, how important and how crucial

SACRIFICE is because of his markings. His markings separate him from all the rest of the trees and they always have and they always will. Legacy finally comprehends why SACRIFICE told him that even he could be cut down some day, but not for the reasons the other trees were marked or cut down. Other trees rob other trees and keep them from bearing fruit. They spread diseases among other trees. They damage others by polluting them with false information, especially about SACRIFICE.

    Legacy realizes the old world deceived him many times. Those in the old world told him there's no use trying to get out of here. They told him you're better off just staying here. They told him, "you can't make it in that world without us, so why even try." They told him in the other world, "there's no reason for you to change." Legacy knows these were all lies now. He knows the other world deceived him. He knows it is this deception that kept him in darkness longer than he needed to be. Yet Legacy had something deep inside him that made him keep pushing upward, though he didn't know it at that time. It's knowing.

Now, Legacy knows the truth. The truth is SACRIFICE is always with you. He never leaves you. He's never missing. He's everywhere. He sees all things. He truly knows all things. He keeps every one of his promises. Legacy just had to come to believe that SACRIFICE is eternal. He had to reach a place of knowing. And he has finally reached that place. He's reached that place within himself that he knows, that he knows, that he knows, that SACRIFICE is the ETERNAL SACRIFICE for Legacy and for every tree in the land. He knows that once a tree accepts SACRIFICE for himself, its name will change as he did also. He knows he can as well as other trees can live forever and stand tall like SACRIFICE. He knows when this happens you will have real joy. Unspeakable Joy.

Legacy knows SACRIFICE is the only tree that can save all other trees. Because he knows he has the responsibility to help other trees know the truth. He knows he has the responsibility to help others know their worth. As he ponders these things, Legacy says to himself, "I've got to make sure every generation knows about SACRIFICE."

Then he proclaims to the world so loud and with such boldness to all nature and all creation especially, to all the trees on the mountains and to all the trees in the valley hear him say, "OLD TREE is SACRIFICE, the TREE OF LIFE, THE SAVIOUR OF ALL TREES." "HE IS THE TREE THAT MAKES IT POSSIBLE FOR ME TO LIVE AND TO KEEP ON LIVING FOREVER." "AND HE WILL MAKE IT POSSIBLE FOR YOU TO LIVE

FOREVER IF YOU TOO ACCEPT HIM."

On this day, the day he said, "YES" Legacy knows he has learned some valuable lessons. SACRIFICED himself so others can live. Legacy has learned that SACRIFICE is indeed "The ETERNAL SACRIFICE." He has learned that although other trees have made SACRIFICE before and others will make future sacrifices, none of these sacrifices will be greater than those of SACRIFICE.

Legacy expresses his love for SACRIFICE. Then he asks, SACRIFICE to forgive him for walking in fear. He asks SACRIFICE to forgive him for doubting him. He asks SACRIFICE to forgive him for not having faith to believe in him. Then he asks SACRIFICE to forgive him for not believing in himself and his own worth.

Legacy knows three undeniable facts, "no," three undeniable truths:

1. SACRIFICE was before the beginning and beyond the end.

2. SACRIFICE lives in our heart by love.

3. Just because SACRIFICE doesn't answer you right away doesn't mean he is not listening. He will answer at the appointed and appropriate time.

Then Legacy vows that every generation for a thousand generations to come will know who SACRIFICE was and still is and who SACRIFICE will always be.

So Legacy drops seeds of righteousness along the paths wherever new ground is moist enough to receive them like water dripping from a water spout.

The Author
Peggy B. Dixon

Peggy Dixon is a woman of integrity. She is a gifted teacher and conference speaker. She is a powerful prophetic woman of God. You see this gift activated when she preaches and teaches. She is a marriage investor. She makes these investments when she holds marriage conferences, as she provides sound wisdom, good advice, counseling, and insight from the WORD of GOD as well as her own marital experiences. She is the author of the book MEATLOAF & MARRIAGE, What Do They Have in Common? She is often found saying, "Marriage is work but it is also worth it." She is known affectionately as a Pearl of Great Price. She believes all women everywhere are "Pearls," you just have to look deep enough to find it.

Her most recent women's conference held the title, "A Strand of Pearls," speaking to women that we are all single pearls separately but when we come together putting aside our differences and when we come to understand how much we need each other we can produce "A Strand of Pearls." Though she speaks to women groups, she is not limited to them. One of her greatest desires is to see *men* be just that: *men*, accepting the responsibility that comes with manhood. She believes if she can help men to understand the role of manhood, she may just as well help save a family union. It's her experiences and her boldness that enable her to strengthen others as she plants seeds of hope to those she comes in contact with. Peggy resides in Louisville, Kentucky with her husband, Walter R. Dixon, of forty-six years. They have two daughters, Reesa and Rachel

Dixon, and one son and daughter-in law, Cyrus and Stephanie Dixon.

They are blessed with grandsons: Darnell, Joel, little brother Timothy, Twins: Walter and Wesley, and the memory of Israel.

Author's Other Book

MEATLOAF AND MARRIAGE

What Do They Have in Common?

Contact the Author

pegggybrucedixon@gmail.com

YOU ARE THE LEGACY: A GENERATIONAL TREE

YOU ARE THE LEGACY: A GENERATIONAL TREE will help you find the truth.

YOU ARE THE LEGACY: A GENERATIONAL TREE gives one a new perspective on life.

YOU ARE THE LEGACY: A GENERATIONAL TREE provides provoking experiences to help you evaluate your own life experiences.

YOU ARE THE LEGACY: A GENERATIONAL TREE offers directions and insights.

YOU ARE THE LEGACY: A GENERATIONAL TREE is challenging because it introduces you to yourself.

YOU ARE THE LEGACY: A GENERAL TREE answers questions as it makes you question yourself.

YOU ARE THE LEGACY: A GENERATIONAL TREE gives one new vision.

www.ingramcontent.com/pod-product-compliance
Lightning Source LLC
Chambersburg PA
CBHW071221160426
43196CB00012B/2363